# WHISPER

## OF THE

# Wings

12 LESSONS REVEALED BY
THE BUTTERFLY LIFE CYCLE

# WHISPER

## OF THE

# *Wings*

KARMON MILLER HILL

# DEDICATION

*To my mom, the most beautiful butterfly in human form. Thank you for seeing my potential well before I ever could and for pushing me until I, too, could see it.*

*To Marvin. Thank you for a marriage overflowing with love, laughter, patience (lots of it), and encouragement.*

*To Kam. Thank you for always being my cheerleader, my sounding board, and my wonder twin power.*

*Last, this book is dedicated to those who have said over the years, "You should write a book." Well, here it is. I hope you love it as much as I have loved writing it for you.*

*The Lord said, "Go out and stand on the mountain in the presence of
the Lord, for the Lord is about to pass by."*

*Then a great and powerful wind tore the mountains apart and shattered the
rocks before the Lord, but the Lord was not in the wind. After the wind there
was an earthquake, but the Lord was not in the earthquake.
After the earthquake came a fire, but the Lord was not in the fire. And after
the fire came a gentle whisper.*

1 Kings 19:11-12

*First Edition*
ISBN: 979-8-9925659-0-4

Self-published by Karmon Miller Hill
Printed in the United States of America

All images photographed by the author with the following exceptions:
page 14, black swallowtail eggs on fennel by Mark Kostich,
page 20, black swallowtail – first instar by Diaa Bekheet

Scripture quotations are taken from the Holy Bible, New Living Translation, copyright ©1978, 1983 by Tyndale House Foundation. Used by permission of Tyndale House Publishers, Carol Stream, Illinois 60188. All rights reserved.

This book is for informational and inspirational purposes only. The author makes no representations or warranties regarding the completeness, accuracy, or applicability of the contents.
The information is not intended as professional, legal, medical, or financial advice. Readers are encouraged to seek professional guidance where appropriate.

Cover Design by Christian Storm
Book Design by @BeaReisCustodio
Edited by Elizabeth M. Charlé
Author Photo by Carla Taylor Photography @ctshootsu

# CONTENTS

# INTRODUCTION

Where do you go when you need a place to calm your mind—when you physically and mentally feel the weight of the world on your shoulders? In what space can you rejoice, regardless of your circumstances? How do you begin to heal from pain, hurt, insecurity, anxiety, fear, loneliness, anger and other joy-blockers?

When I was experiencing some of these same feelings, I had recently moved and started a new job. Anxiety became my constant companion. I had to find a way to release all that negative energy. Enter, my butterfly garden and the butterflies assigned to share their lessons with me.

From the first summer I built a garden, I began reaping its life-giving benefits in ways I never expected. The word I used to describe my garden and the butterflies that visited was *therapeutic*. I watched, studied, and took mental notes of my observations.

Over time, I started writing down life lessons that emerged at every stage of the butterfly's life cycle. Consider this book the culmination of time spent examining their lives—and my own. I hope the stories and poetry I have written will guide you through the experience of looking inward and finding your inner light. I pray that the lessons revealed by the butterflies bring you a peace that surpasses life's stressors.

This book speaks to the intersection of nature and spirituality. It is, in fact, a book written to honor my Christian walk. If that is not your path, feel free to internalize the ideas in this book through the lens of whatever higher source you acknowledge. There is room for everyone on this journey. I wish you joy and peace as we travel this road together. May the flutter of a butterfly's wings remind you of the gentle whisper that directs us along our path.

# EGG AND CATERPILLAR STAGE

# God Hears the Prayers of Our Heart

Silent whispers, trails of tears.
I cry to you. Do you even hear me?
I lay on your operating table, exposed.
You begin to perform open heart surgery.
Beep.
I love you, my child.
Beep.
I hear your heart.
Beep.
Rest in me and know that I am.
Beep.
Rise. You have been restored.

# LESSON 1

# GOD HEARS THE PRAYERS OF OUR HEART

*This is the confidence we have in approaching God: That if we ask anything according to his will, he hears us.*

1 John 5:14

I love nature, especially insects. If it jumps, crawls, flies, sneak-attacks other bugs, or can spit toxins from ten feet away, it's got my attention; however, of all the insects in the world, there is a clear and uncontested winner that steals my heart: butterflies.

I have always loved butterflies, but when I relocated to a different state, I realized I had taken them for granted, particularly monarchs. Once I moved, I quickly noticed there were times when I never saw monarchs, and other times they magically took over the city during their migratory trek. The monarch migration was a beautiful sight to witness. When they arrived, their big, beautiful, orange and black wings would flap boldly against the wind, everywhere I turned. When the light caught them just right, it was like watching little pieces of stained-glass fluttering in the sky.

As a result, I created a garden space to attract the monarchs, filling it with milkweed in hopes to see a few. A few weeks after I planted what I had hoped to be a butterfly oasis, we made the decision to move. I was so disappointed. I hoped the next person to live in our home would nurture my newly established garden. I even attached a copper-colored metal plaque, engraved with multicolored flowers and curly green letters that read "Butterfly Garden," to the fence so the next residents would hopefully recognize how special this space was. Though sad to leave the garden behind, I knew God would eventually give me the garden of my dreams ... maybe not then and there, but eventually.

In addition to leaving my newly planted garden, nothing in my life seemed to be going right at this time. A promotion I had hoped for was stalled, and it seemed like there was constant pushback. Work seemed to be never-ending. My marriage had taken a backseat to work, and I couldn't figure out how to give it the time it deserved. Also, I started to notice health concerns with a loved one that had me worried.

Overall, my mental state and physical health were under daily attack. I felt like I was in a valley. During this period, I prayed fervently, sharing both my worries and the desires of my heart with God. Despite this season (which seemed to have no end), I could feel God's presence. The best way to describe the presence of the Almighty is a feeling of anticipation combined with hope, securely wrapped in a blanket of love and grace. It's like that feeling you get when someone says, "I got you," and you know and trust that you will be taken care of and have nothing to worry about.

But I must relay, there were some dark days. Sometimes God uses our circumstances to accomplish his will. God didn't just say, "Here you go. Have an easy life." He didn't wave a magic wand. There was no perfect health diagnosis for my loved one. "No more worries, no more pain" was not the motto of the day. But, God brought every prayer for which I petitioned to fruition ... not always in my time or the way I expected it to look, which we will discuss later, but he heard each one. He will do the same for you. Why? Because God hears the prayers of our hearts. Yes. All of them. Even the crazy ones that anticipate a flourishing butterfly garden.

That job promotion you want? He hears. The healing you asked for in your body? That, too. Joy in your marriage? Indeed. Peace and deliverance from circumstances out of your control? Yep. He hears you. Prayers for your children and family members? Most definitely.

When your desires align with God's plans for your life, there is no stopping what God has for you. Even in your struggles, God's unwavering love is near. Breathe. He hears the prayers of your heart. He hears the prayers that you pray for others. Be still and surrender and know that God is in control.

1. What prayer in your heart do you want God to hear?

2. What have been some prayers God has answered for you or someone you prayed for?

3. Read these scriptures. Do these help you to feel more confident that God hears the prayers of your heart?

   Matthew 7:7 *Ask, and it will be given to you; seek, and you will find; knock, and the door will be opened to you.*

   Psalm 34:15 *The eyes of the LORD are on the righteous, and his ears are attentive to their cry.*

   Ephesians 6:18-20 *And pray in the Spirit on all occasions with all kinds of prayers and requests. With this in mind, be alert and always keep on praying for all the Lord's people. Pray also for me, that whenever I speak, words may be given me so that I will fearlessly make known the mystery of the gospel, for which I am an ambassador in chains. Pray that I may declare it fearlessly, as I should.*

# LESSON 1 NOTES

## POEM 2

# God's Time Is Not Our Time

Winter becomes spring.
Spring becomes summer, then fall.
God takes no shortcuts.

# LESSON 2

# GOD'S TIME IS NOT OUR TIME

*He said to them: "It is not for you to know the times or dates the Father has set by his own authority."*
Acts 1:7

❧

Operation Butterfly Oasis was underway the spring after we moved. Determined to have butterflies circling around my yard, I spent hours researching plants and flowers that different butterflies used for nectar and to lay eggs. I researched the life cycle, migratory pattern, and everything imaginable. I was Mother Butterfly!

With plans in hand, I opted for milkweed and fennel, which were host plants for monarch butterflies and black swallowtail butterflies. This plan of mine seemed easy enough ... plant and water, then sit back and watch the butterflies come swarming through. WRONG! I saw not ONE butterfly in my garden. To make things worse, I didn't see butterflies anywhere in our new neighborhood! This butterfly worshiper was beyond disappointed.

Each day, I peered out the back door with anticipation, and each day, I was met with the same reality. Not one butterfly. This went on day after day, week after week. One day, I walked over to my little garden to take inventory, as I did every morning. I could not believe what I saw! I counted about ten small black swallowtail caterpillars on my fennel plant! I was SHOCKED. What I learned was, yes, God answers the prayers of our heart when there is alignment, but also, God does it in his time. This is a hard thing to know and even harder to execute. God's timetable is not on our schedule.

Back to the stalled job promotion I mentioned in the last chapter—that was not on my timetable either. I tried to wait patiently, but I just knew I was ready. I wondered why God didn't see that. I think the answer is twofold. One, he has a bigger picture and wider lens than I do. More importantly, there is growth and discipline involved in waiting, and he wants us to fully give him the glory once the answer is yes.

I am happy to report I did get a promotion, but a full year later than I wanted! The promotion saga began when I decided I wanted to become a senior in the role I performed. But, to become a senior, you had to first lead a project. In November of that year, I was given the opportunity to lead a project. It was supposed to be a nice, short project and then done. I worked on the project and then delivered it by January. Great. Done. Now where's my promotion? Not so fast I was told. All people they were looking at for promotions that year had already been selected, and I would need to wait until the end of the year, which would allow me to possibly get a promotion the next year. I was devastated. Begrudgingly, I moved through the year.

An interesting thing happened. My project morphed and got larger and larger. I had to take on more, learn some things along the way, experience and recover from scheduling snafus and failure, and prove myself for a second year in a row at pulling off a flawless meeting. And you know what? Not only did I do all these things, but as I did them, I felt myself grow in confidence, I felt myself grow in leadership, and I felt myself grow in knowing how to own and fix issues that arose. In short, I was no longer just checking things off a list, but I began to embrace the spirit of the process behind the things I was tasked with doing. I became more strategic. I learned how to lead not just a project, but also a team. I learned how to deal with ambiguity, and how to make valuable suggestions that helped meet our clients' needs.

Had I gotten the promotion a year earlier, if I were being honest with myself, I could not have said I knew how to lead a project. That year of growth, though not my plan, was God's plan to make me stronger, wiser, and more confident ... and to learn how to truly exercise that so-called faith I had. The day I presented my case for promotion to the committee, and then the day I received my promotion, were two days I felt most accomplished in my professional career.

Time does not always seem to be our friend, but God always is. Romans 8:25 states, "But if we hope for what we do not see, we wait for it with patience." We must never forget that God does answer prayers, but in his time. Rest in assurance. Your day is coming.

1. What if God's response is, "Wait." What are some things you can do while in the waiting mode?

2. Why is it so hard for us to be patient? Does being impatient mean we don't trust God?

3. Read these scriptures. How can these help during the waiting period?

   Galatians 6:9 *Let us not become weary in doing good, for at the proper time we will reap a harvest if we do not give up.*

   Romans 12:12 *Be joyful in hope, patient in affliction, faithful in prayer.*

   Lamentations 3:25-26 *The Lord is good to those whose hope is in him, to the one who seeks him; it is good to wait quietly for the salvation of the Lord.*

# LESSON 2 NOTES

POEM 3

# We Should Be in Community

A funeral procession inches by
like ants with their marching orders.
Cars on the left pull over,
one, then many,
until they, too, had formed their own procession
of respectful stillness, for a person unknown.
Realization strikes.
In the end, we all have
at least one thing in common–
And that should be enough.

# LESSON 3

# WE SHOULD BE IN COMMUNITY

*And let us consider how we may spur one another on toward love and good deeds, not giving up meeting together, as some are in the habit of doing, but encouraging one another—and all the more as you see the Day approaching.*
Hebrews 10:24-25

I watched the caterpillars grow. In the mornings, they seemed to cluster nearby. It was almost like they had a sense of community. Whether it was instinctual to keep warm or from being eaten by predators, or for other reasons, it was clear to see that nature gathered them together during one of their most vulnerable times—when they rested at night. I would see them, nestled near each other right before the light, and heat of the day made them active. They seemed to understand the adage "there is security in numbers."

Like the caterpillars, we need community as well. I have three amazing communities that have been my lifeline. Each one serves a different need.

The first group I found when I was a stay-at-home mom. I remembered the feeling of isolation I felt when I had my first son. I was so lonely, like inside looking out and wondering why everyone else was so happy on a sunny day, and why I was so sad. When I gave birth to my second son, I immediately searched for a group where my children and I could connect with others. I remember calling to inquire, and the president telling me they had taken a hiatus but were just getting the group back together. That was all I needed to hear. I joined Mocha Moms two weeks later. Through this group, I not only had a great group of playmates for my children, but ladies who have become lifelong friends. I recall attending the second meeting, where I met a very sweet lady. At the end of the meeting, she told me, "I think we're going to be friends for a long time." She was right. To this day, she is one of my best friends. We get together over tea to enjoy each other's company every few weeks. We have been there for each other in good times and bad, and her presence in my life has been a Godsend. I can say the same about so many of the other ladies. Oh, the laughter and joy we experience around each other!

I am also part of an amazing community of seven other women. Together, we are known as the Stone Canyon Sistahs. When I say we do life together, we DO life together. We have been together for the last twenty-plus years. We all moved into our original neighborhood around the same time and have rallied as a collective unit to witness births, deaths, divorces, graduations, new jobs, and family events. We share meals and laughs at each other's house and bust some moves on the carpet in each other's living rooms. We are the aunties to each other's children, and daughters to each other's parents. When the last of us is left standing, we will truly be able to say the Stone Canyon Sistahs were shining examples of friends who are indeed family.

The last community of significance is my church family. These have been very special groups of men and women with whom I do life inside and outside of church. These are the ones that help to make the church not feel so large and impersonal. These are also people with whom I pray, who pray for me, and who hold me accountable, with convicted love.

One person in particular, Beverly, has become like a sister to me. We enjoy each other's company, and every time we see each other at church, we sit together and take a selfie afterwards. It is her thing to get a selfie of us, and it makes me smile inwardly each time we do. It is safe to say that with a heart as beautiful as hers, there is little I would not do for her if she asked.

Being in community requires that we show up. A few years ago, Beverly's brother passed away. His funeral was in a town about an hour away from where I lived, down a back road that made me uncomfortable. But I kept driving, because I knew my presence there would mean a lot to her. Sure enough, she smiled with a surprised look on her face when she saw me and came over at the end to give me a big hug and tell me how grateful she was I came. I told her it was my pleasure. It was a blessing to show up for her the way she shows up for me and so many others.

When it comes to community there are those who think they can survive without it. Sure, you can ... but the question is, do you want to survive, or do you want to thrive? Open your doors and your heart. It will bless both you and the ones you let enter.

1. Do you have any trust issues that make it difficult to be in community? How do you think God is preparing your heart to move from not trusting to believing in the power of community?

2. Do you wait for others to create community? What can you do to foster connections inside your community and inside your church?

3. Read these scriptures. Do they change or validate your ideas about community?

   Matthew 18:20 *For where two or three gather in my name, there am I with them.*

   Galatians 6:2 *Carry each other's burdens, and in this way you will fulfill the law of Christ.*

   Acts 2:42-47 *They devoted themselves to the apostles' teaching and to fellowship, to the breaking of bread and to prayer. Everyone was filled with awe at the many wonders and signs performed by the apostles. All the believers were together and had everything in common. They sold property and possessions to give to anyone who had need. Every day they continued to meet together in the temple courts. They broke bread in their homes and ate together with glad and sincere hearts, praising God and enjoying the favor of all the people. And the Lord added to their number daily those who were being saved.*

# LESSON 3 NOTES

## POEM 4

# God Wants Us to Grow in Him

Wade in the water with me.
Take my hand as we move to where dreams swirl
  deeper;
beyond the sand seen through water washing onto
  the shore.
Wade with me into high tide
as we swim out to where the ocean greets us,
rich with possibilities.

# LESSON 4
# GOD WANTS US TO GROW IN HIM

*Therefore if anyone is in Christ, the new creation has come.*
*The old has gone, the new is here!*
2 Corinthians 5:17

⁓

I loved what was happening in my garden. I was amazed at how big my caterpillars seemed to grow from day to day. The caterpillars grew like little giants, spending just a short time in their "new" bodies, only to have them replaced by newer, bigger ones. If I looked closely, I would sometimes notice what looked like a dried-up old casing stuck to some of the leaves. I read that some caterpillars will molt (shed their skin) five times to accommodate this rapid growth. Each of these molts grows the caterpillar to its next instar (period of development). I found it so interesting and poetic that the caterpillars didn't stay right by their old skin. They were off to live their best lives in their newly formed skin. It was as if the old was indeed left in the past, and their only focus was continuing to grow and develop.

While caterpillars grow physically, we as humans can grow in other ways. I have had five growth periods that have profoundly placed me on the path I am on. My first period of growth as an adult came when I went to college. This was the time I chose to get baptized. I had believed in Christ my entire life, but this was my time to make the outward declaration as we are called to do. It was clearly the best decision I have made to date.

My second period of growth came when I accepted my first job out of school. I learned how to truly live on my own, be content by myself, and turn plans into action. This was the time I was mostly alone with my thoughts and God. This time offered me a period of profound rest and trusting in God.

My third period of growth came when I decided to leave my first job to pursue graduate studies full time. I learned how to lean on God when I had setbacks with my projects and relationships. Also, I learned how to talk to God and seek his counsel for decisions I made, which led to me dating a wonderful man who is now my husband.

My fourth period of growth came when I became a mom. I remember the overwhelming feeling of having another life completely dependent on me. I learned to lean on God's counsel. Then three and a half years later, I had my second child. I learned the truest meaning of God's grace and mercy with my second-born, who was a much tougher child. I learned to extend this same grace and mercy God extends to us.

Now, I am in my fifth period of growth. This is a very important period for me, because I am learning to grow in the gifts God has given me. I am blessed to have two gifts. My first gift is teaching others. I used to be a middle school math teacher, and I loved imparting knowledge to my students! The biggest reward was to see their faces light up when they "got it." I have also been a fourth and fifth grade Sunday school teacher for many years. I love teaching students about the Word of God, so that they may eventually grow up to accept Christ for themselves. I was also given the gift of communicating. There became a voice inside telling me to write my story, so here we are. I continue to honor God's voice in my writing. My biggest prayer is that what I write will bless the lives of others, while honoring God's purpose for my life. I pray to have many more periods of growth throughout my life.

It is important for us to continue to grow. Imagine if God is trying to grow you and expand your mind, yet you keep the same shallow thoughts as you had before you knew him. He would have no room to work, and you would have no room to grow.

Growth is not always easy, but like each stage the caterpillar goes through, it is necessary to shed our old thoughts, our old lives, our old habits, and sometimes even our old friends, to reach our full potential. The sooner we surrender and move through the process of growing, especially spiritually, the quicker we are able to experience the fullness of the life God wants to offer us.

1. Name an area in which you would like to grow.

2. What actions, big or small, are you doing to get to that place?

3. What do you think about the fact that you can trust God to help you grow in those areas? How do these scriptures help to align your thinking?

John 15:5 *I am the vine; you are the branches. If you remain in me and I in you, you will bear much fruit; apart from me you can do nothing.*

Peter 2:2-3 *Like newborn babies, crave spiritual milk so that by it you may grow up in your salvation, now that you have tasted that the Lord is good.*

Proverbs 1:5 *Let the wise listen and add to their learning, and let the discerning get guidance.*

# LESSON 4 NOTES

# PUPA (CHRYSALIS) STAGE

## POEM 5

# Finding God in Isolation and Transformation

Isolated from
noise of the world's distractions,
a transformative
process of flesh and spirit–
God desires to mold us.

# LESSON 5

# FINDING GOD IN ISOLATION AND TRANSFORMATION

*Do not conform to the pattern of this world, but be transformed by the renewing of your mind. Then you will be able to test and approve what God's will is—his good, pleasing and perfect will.*

Romans 12:2

Each year, my beautiful garden continued to flourish. Over a three-year period, I had provided a safe haven for three different types of caterpillars—black swallowtail the first year, gulf fritillary the second, and monarchs the third. Each time, the caterpillars grew long and thick.

My greatest joy was to walk out to my garden each morning and throughout the day. I had begun to understand their routine well and could pinpoint about when it was time for them to leave the bush. Admittedly, the first year, I was beyond confused when the first was not on the bush but was instead on the ground moving intently toward the grass. Thinking it was lost or confused, I put it back on the bush. But later, I saw two following that same path. It became clear to me they were leaving the safety of numbers and their leafy haven to seek a new space for the transformation they were about to undergo. This was not a group activity, but an individual event, where they would go to a spot to begin the miraculous process of transforming from a caterpillar to a butterfly.

Nature has a beautiful way of becoming what it is intended to be. Similarly, there are times where we require isolation to transform into who God intends us to be.

When I first graduated from college, I accepted a job that required me to live in a remote place. When I moved to this town of 5,000 people, if I wanted to visit someone, I had to practically drive through cornfields to see them ... a new experience indeed! It was so small that everyone knew who I was and where I lived. One time I invited a guest to visit me. I told her to let me know when she got close so I could guide her to my place. Imagine my surprise when she showed up. I asked, "How did you get here?" Her response: "The guy at the gas station told me where to find you." Not creepy, right? The point is, this was a "where everybody knows your name" kind of small place. But, despite the different culture of this town, I thrived.

I had my first apartment which was at a new apartment complex. Beautiful and peaceful, it was a modern townhouse style apartment with my own garage. I have always valued silence, so the quietness never bothered me. It left me alone with my thoughts, and I never had to take work home, so I had little stress. Everyone at the factory where I worked left for home at 4:30, and no one expected me to be on the clock a minute later. In short, I was isolated. The byproduct was that it gave my mind space to breathe and grow. I spent a lot of time with God. I prayed, read devotionals, listened to Christian music, and spent a lot of time listening. I didn't entirely love the town where I lived, especially in the winter, but I loved the solace I received from this time of isolation.

When it warmed up after that first winter, I decided to visit my friend. It was a fun visit, but fast paced and busy. Confession—I rescheduled my flight and went home a day early, just to get back to a calmer state. While I was on the plane, the lady next to me and I had a great conversation. Her faith was evident from the minute we spoke. I told her about going home early and being relieved to soon be back in the peace and tranquility of my space. I told her about being isolated from everyone where I lived, and that only one person had come to visit, given the location and the weather.

What she said to me profoundly shook my world, and I have never forgotten that conversation. She said, "Maybe God wanted to get you alone to have this time for you to focus and spend time with him." She could not have been more correct. My faith grew, and I could feel God directing my path.

As an act of faith, I decided to quit my job and go back to school full time to pursue a graduate degree. As part of God's plan, I was able to apply for a severance package at work which helped pay for my move and rent, find funding for school, work with the advisor I wanted, and find a bubbly, Christ-centered roommate who was entering the same program.

This same faith continued to be my source of strength on some of the hardest days academically that followed. After many trials, tears, and prayers, I completed my graduate degree with honors. As a bonus, I met an amazing man who has been my wonderful husband for over twenty-five years.

My time in isolation transformed my faith, my faith turned into a reliance on God, and my reliance has allowed me to be still and know that he is God. It is in silence and isolation that you can hear God's voice the loudest.

1. Can you reflect on a time when you felt isolated and alone?

2. How would this time have felt if you used it to spend time reading, praying, and listening to God? If you did use it as time to read, pray, and listen, what did you learn?

3. Read the scriptures shared below. In what ways does being alone with God help us to connect? How did Jesus model the need for isolation and alone time?

   Matthew 6:6 *But when you pray, go into your room, close the door and pray to your Father, who is unseen. Then your Father, who sees what is done in secret, will reward you.*

   Luke 5:16 *But Jesus often withdrew to lonely places and prayed.*

   Psalm 62:1 *Truly my soul finds rest in God; my salvation comes from him.*

# LESSON 5 NOTES

POEM 6

# You Do Not Look Like What You've Been Through

I am the guest of honor at the masquerade ball.
What is beneath this mask would draw pity from
   some
and tears from others—
but I know the Truth.
The great reveal is in the making
by the great I AM.

# LESSON 6

# YOU DO NOT LOOK LIKE WHAT YOU'VE BEEN THROUGH

*Keep me safe, Lord, from the hands of the wicked; protect me from the violent, who devise ways to trip my feet.*
Psalm 140:4

When the weather cooled down, I had the privilege of having three caterpillars become chrysalises. This meant I was tasked with keeping them alive through the winter (though the truth is, like God, they probably didn't need my help). Two caterpillars had formed their chrysalises inside of my butterfly net. But one of caterpillars had attached itself to a brick as it began its transformation to becoming a chrysalis. The caterpillar had barely begun its change when I accidentally knocked the brick on the side where the chrysalis was forming. After standing the brick back up, I was sure this caterpillar could not have survived. But two days later, I noticed it had become a chrysalis. This chrysalis, however, didn't look smooth and defined like the two others. It looked more like a piece of rugged wood. Weeks passed with no issues, until I woke up one night because of a thunderstorm. My first thought was, "Oh no, what about my chrysalises?" I went outside to check. The two that were at the top of the butterfly net were fine. However, the chrysalis on the brick was soaked. Again, I wondered if its butterfly journey had been cut short. And then there was the frost. This poor chrysalis had gone through so much, ragged outer layer and all. I just could not imagine how it could have survived all these instances.

The weather began to warm, and one late February day in Texas, the first butterfly emerged. Fast forward to late March, and the second butterfly emerged from its sleep, ready to take flight.

The only one left was this pitiful, bark-like chrysalis that had been crushed, soaked, and frozen. My honest expectation was that this would not be a viable butterfly, but I kept it, nonetheless. To my absolute delight and surprise, two weeks later, I saw a beautiful, vibrant, active black swallowtail flying around inside the net, its former place of protection split wide open! This butterfly emerged victorious from all the circumstances that it had gone through.

I have a friend whose life story is very similar to that butterfly that had been crushed, soaked, and frozen. Her life would be considered by most as tragic and painful, wrought with males harming her and females not protecting her. Growing up, her home life was not stable. She had a mom who loved her and gave her a great start, but who had herself endured a fractured past.

As a result, my friend had to grow up very quickly. Before the age of 10, she was taking public transportation to get to school. At some point, she and her mom had to vacate their apartment. When this happened, my friend moved without her mom to her grandmother's house. She was poorly treated there and was eventually made to leave that residence She then went to stay with her paternal grandmother. Other family members lived in the house, including several cousins and an uncle, who began having inappropriate relations with her. This went on for years. When she had the courage to tell, her story was dismissed and she was ostracized by her family.

Heartbreaking. My friend picked up the pieces after this betrayal, and the betrayal of many more men who should have protected her. Through her will and determination, she finished high school, still taking public transportation daily to a place nowhere near where she resided. She then put herself through college, and eventually grad school. Most could not have made it through her journey. But my friend is not like anyone I know. Some would ask, "How could God do this?" but the truth is, there is hurt and pain in the world. Even in this madness, God carved out a safe space to protect her mental capacity and gave her the will to survive.

He allowed her to navigate the uncharted, treacherous waters of life. Her trust in God has allowed her to minister to others who are hurting and in need of help. She shares stories of God's unfailing love to all who will listen. She is standing strong and is now working to complete her doctorate studies on a topic close to her heart. If "I don't look like what I've been through" were a person, she'd be the poster child. I could not be prouder of my friend who I consider a sister.

1. How do you feel about what others think or say about you? Why or why not?

2. What do you believe God sees when he looks at you and the things you've done or gone through?

3. Have you been able to heal from the hurt caused by others? Why or why not?

4. Read the following scriptures. How does this change or reinforce the way God sees you?

Ephesians 2:4-5 *But because of his great love for us, God, who is rich in mercy, made us alive with Christ even when we were dead in transgressions—it is by grace you have been saved.*

Isaiah 43:4 *Since you are precious and honored in my sight, and because I love you, I will give people in exchange for you, nations in exchange for your life.*

Psalm 139:13-14 *For you created my inmost being; you knit me together in my mother's womb. I praise you because I am fearfully and wonderfully made; your works are wonderful, I know that full well.*

# LESSON 6 NOTES

POEM 7

# We Must Let Go to Grow

I pulled my coat to button it,
Two sizes too small, it ripped.
I put my shoes on to leave the house,
Two sizes too small, I could not walk.
You placed a new coat and new shoes before me,
But of the new, I did not take.
Content, or at least familiar, with the old,
I continued to squeeze.
One day, I decided to dream.
My dreams made my heart bigger,
My heart made my mind bigger,
My mind made my world bigger.
I could no longer fit in the old,
I shed the old coat and shoes for the new.
Now I dance among the stars,
Free to move, free to dream, free to grow.

# LESSON 7

# WE MUST LET GO TO GROW

*Forget the former things; do not dwell on the past.*
Isaiah 43:18

As mentioned, each year, all the caterpillars set out on a great trek from their original host plants to wherever they decided was the best place for the next phase in their journey. No matter what spot each one selected, the process was the same. The caterpillar would spin a sticky web material to attach its end, it would curl up in a j-shape, and after a day of staying like that, it would form a hard exterior that became a chrysalis.

I would see evidence of that last layer shed, and then in about fourteen days, I would see a beautiful butterfly break through the thinned case that held the secrets to what was transforming inside. Never, not once, at the end of those fourteen days, did a caterpillar emerge. Never once did Mother Nature decide that once transformation started, because of what it was in its past, it should not fulfill its destiny. Yet at times, many of us decide to put that limitation on our lives. Metamorphosis requires a change in mindset and a willingness to leave behind what no longer serves God's purpose for our lives.

Similarly, sometimes courage requires us to leave where we are and to go someplace new in order to grow. I spent nine years at my last job, and I was good at what I did. Even when it required long hours, I was happy with the work and its purpose. I worked with an amazing group of coworkers and had mentored several of our newcomers. At that time, I was considering a move into management. I had become quite comfortable, but I still had a nagging feeling.

This feeling continued to grow. Once my sons were older, I started wondering what life (and finances) would have looked like had I stayed in engineering. I had no regrets staying where I was for nine years, because it allowed me to work from home and be available for my boys. But being that I had earned the degree, I felt led to see if the timing was right for a new plan. I shared my desires with one of my former coworkers at the tech company I had originally been hired at twenty years earlier, and it just so happened there was an opening on their team.

Now the big deal: interviewing. I interviewed with four different people including the manager and director of the team, and guess what? No, I was not hired, because the pandemic hit, and all requisitions were canceled. I was devastated but I still had a job I enjoyed, so I carried on. Fast forward a year, and I reached out again to the same manager to see where things stood. I was informed they were opening back up requisitions, and if I was still interested, I would be hired!

After much prayer, I said, "Yes." Saying yes, I quickly found out, was the easy part. In short, my first few months were TOUGH. I struggled. There were some ideas and concepts in the group that were 'tribal knowledge' that other newcomers and I had to figure out. I had so many questions, and then my questions caused me to have questions. I had to learn who the key players were and the deliverables that were expected. When my first project was handed off to me in a shorter time than I anticipated, I felt like I was not ready. There was so much to learn.

Day by day, I struggled to find my way. I shed lots of tears and felt the highest level of impostor syndrome possible. But I kept praying and crying, and praying and crying, and I just kept moving forward. A year passed, and I noticed something about myself I didn't notice the year prior—I had gone from knowing very little to being able to explain some things. Then the next year I went from being able to explain a few things to being able to offer suggestions. I'm now about to enter a new year, and I feel like I have grown by leaps and bounds over this past year to where I share thoughts and answers with more confidence. It has not been an easy path, but this was the next step I was looking for in life: to find a challenge where I could constantly grow as I lean on God to make me the best version of me. He has delivered on this challenge and then some.

1. Write down people or situations you know you need to let go of in order to grow.

2. Sometimes we want to control situations instead of letting God handle them. What do you struggle to let go of?

3. What do these scriptures say about letting go of people and situations that no longer serve you, and of letting go of control?

   Isaiah 43:19 *See, I am doing a new thing! Now it springs up; do you not perceive it? I am making a way in the wilderness and streams in the wasteland.*

   Proverbs 3:5-6 *Trust in the Lord with all your heart and lean not on your own understanding; in all your ways submit to him, and he will make your paths straight.*

   Peter 5:7 *Cast all your anxiety on him because he cares for you.*

# LESSON 7 NOTES

# POEM 8

## We Must Be Patient During Transition

Persistent patience
delays gratification
until the right time.

# LESSON 8
# WE MUST BE PATIENT DURING TRANSITION

*You need to persevere so that when you have done the will of God, you will receive what he has promised.*
Hebrews 10:36

The journey of the butterfly, from egg to butterfly, is an exercise in patience. It is a journey that can neither be rushed nor shortened. From the first egg I saw on the plant, to the teeny wiggling, barely recognizable baby caterpillars, to the fat caterpillars that had shed multiple times, to the pupa stage, to the butterflies emerging … or waiting all winter before emerging … all represented the essence of patience.

It had nothing to do with what the caterpillars wanted. There were no negotiations to speed up the process or make the tough parts shorter than the easy parts. Each phase and transition was tuned to nature's clock. Like the caterpillars, we, too, should surrender and trust the process.

The birth of my second child was a true blessing—a beautiful, healthy baby. What I didn't realize, however, was this was going to be both my biggest challenge and my biggest reward. I recognized early on that he had some academic struggles.

His preschool teacher expressed concern when he was four. I had been home with him since he was born, so I was able to see some of the concerns that were expressed. A year passed, and it was time to consider kindergarten. But my heart wasn't settled that this was the right choice for him.

After discussion with my husband, we decided to give him an extra year in the program he was at, rather than start him in kindergarten. I slept better than I had slept in a long time that evening after making that decision. He spent the next year growing, developing, and being nurtured. It was truly great to see him develop, but I still noticed some struggles.

We spent the summer before kindergarten continuing to get ready. Kindergarten came. He was doing okay, but in talking to his teacher there were still concerns in his ability to do the work.

We opted for him to get assistance in the areas of reading and math to get the support he needed. With a plan in place and dedicated teachers, my son moved along. He made notable strides as we all continued to put in the time and effort. One big challenge was in fourth grade, when he would take his first state-wide writing test. He had an amazingly strong teacher, Ms. Rod. I had heard from a reliable source, my oldest son, that if I wanted his brother to become a strong writer, Ms. Rod was the best. My 'source' was right! My son, after many years of struggling to write well, passed the writing part of his test!

My son would go on to take test after test and sometimes pass the first time, and sometimes need to retake and pass the second time. But he was doing it! He continued with support through middle school, where he learned how to advocate for himself. We moved school districts during middle school, and all the prep and training he had seemed to propel him. He needed assistance less and less and passed several of his tests on the first try. He was a great math student when he put his mind to it and could do mental math better than anyone I know.

Then, at the end of his last year in middle school, everything came to a halt—the pandemic. My son spent his first year online, and it was tough. But he did it. Sophomore year came, and school was in person. Little by little, he started making his way in high school, both academically and socially. His amazing counselor kept him in line, and he met another teacher who became like a second mom to him. My son had progressed so much that by his junior year, everyone agreed that he would no longer need the assistance he had been getting.

As high school wound down, my son made honor roll his last two semesters because he had set a goal to get his GPA to at least a 3.0. His final GPA? 3.1. He was accepted into college and started in the fall. His first semester, he earned a 3.0! Watch out world, he is determined and destined to do great things.

I gave the abridged version—this experience was TOUGH! One thing I learned about both our Father in heaven and my son—they are tougher! The phrase "trust the process" is real, but trusting the process requires real patience. Some journeys take longer than others, but regardless, know that God has a plan and just needs for you to exercise patience, work hard, and trust the process. Your testimony is in the process.

1. Do you ever feel God has forgotten about you or is busy blessing everyone else? How does this make you feel?

2. Sometimes God says, "Yes," sometimes God says, "No." But, sometimes God says, "Wait." What can you do during the times when God says, "Wait"?

3. Read these scriptures. Do these scriptures help you rest easier, knowing that God not only has a plan, but a perfect one?

   Jeremiah 29:11 *For I know the plans I have for you," declares the Lord, "plans to prosper you and not to harm you, plans to give you hope and a future.*

   Romans 8:28 *And we know that in all things God works for the good of those who love him, who have been called according to his purpose.*

   James 1:4 *Let perseverance finish its work so that you may be mature and complete, not lacking anything.*

# LESSON 8 NOTES

# ADULT BUTTERFLY STAGE

POEM 9

# We Must Use Our Gifts

The dream I dream each night I rest
lies just beneath my eyes.
A dream so real that when I wake
it makes me me realize,
I'm born to write, I'm made of words
on wings of words I soar,
to use this voice he placed in me
'til I can speak no more.

# LESSON 9
# WE MUST USE OUR GIFTS

*Each of you should use whatever gift you have received to serve others,*
*as faithful stewards of God's grace in its various forms.*

1 Peter 4:10

One by one, the caterpillars would leave their host plants. Later, I would randomly see evidence of the upcoming transformation they were undergoing when I would see the chrysalis they created. A few weeks later, there it would be! I would see a new butterfly that had broken through its chrysalis sitting there, waiting to pump its wings and fly.

Before the first flight, I could pick the butterfly up, and it would sit on my finger. I would talk to it, look at it, then put it on a flower. After a period of time, the butterfly would take off for its first flight—a beautiful sight to see as it soared to the sky. The butterflies had no fear. They just did what they were designed to do—fly. This is exactly how God designed us to be, if we would take the first step and trust in him. He designed us to soar to our fullest potential. How do we do this? By using the gifts God has given us.

I come from a long line of educators, and I love to teach as well. My first job at sixteen was working as a fourth grade tutor in a classroom. I remember how much I loved the students and equally how much I loved helping them understand the subject matter.

Fast forward to when I was in graduate school, volunteering at the church I attended. I decided I would teach Sunday school. Now here's the funny part: my knowledge of the Bible was not strong besides a few stories I remembered from when I was growing up, but I had the audacity to think I could teach Sunday school.

I remember getting my first lesson. It came with a prayer and walked me through the story and the activity I was to teach. I remember starting out with the prayer and clinging to the prayer as I read the reference notes. As I read the notes for the lesson, a wave of panic came over me. How did I arrive at this crazy idea of thinking that just because I tutored fourth graders, I could somehow share the Bible with students? I kept praying and rereading, because I didn't want to mess up.

The day came. Finally, it was time. I took a deep breath, and began greeting the students as they walked in. They were so sweet! They ranged between eight and nine and were excited to be there. I decided that we would be excited to be there together! You may wonder if the lesson went perfectly. The answer: no. But, we all had a great time learning and laughing together! There were more students than I had anticipated, so my pacing was off, and the room felt too small, but I managed to accommodate everyone.

The lesson came from the Bible story about Jonah and the whale. No clue why that was the first story, but it spoke to me then and continues to speak to me today: when God asks you to do something or tell someone about him, your job is to do it. God has given me many teaching moments since those first Sunday school days. Many years later once I had children, I taught Sunday school again. It started off so I could introduce my sons to children's church, but led to me teaching Sunday school for over fifteen years.

Sometimes God uses one event to prepare you for the next. I have spent a lot of time asking God to increase my territory and give me influence. I used to think that meant outside of the church. Most recently, I have discovered that he is calling me to be inside the church, and to help people better learn about what God is looking for us to do. Imagine how he is calling me to do this ... by using that same gift of teaching.

I have worked as an apprentice, and weekly when I present the lesson, I feel that same anxiety I felt when I first started teaching Sunday school. But what I have come to realize is that God isn't looking for me to be perfect with my lesson each week. He is looking to use me to glorify his name, and to share what a life that's part of the body of Christ looks like.

I'm glad he isn't looking for perfection. Each week the person I am shadowing says or does something that helps me realize I have a lot to learn. But what I do know is that I am helping to be a conduit to change lives, all because I said, "Yes" to being obedient to using the gift God gave me. Think about it this way. What if you gave someone a gift you were so excited to give them, and they never used it? How would you feel? We are to be in relationship with God's family. That requires each of us to learn, open up, be vulnerable, and use the gifts we were given.

1. Have you identified the spiritual gifts given to you by God? If yes, what are they? If not, will you take a test to identify them?

2. How do you use these gifts in your day-to-day life? Are you using them in both your personal and professional life?

3. Read the following scriptures. How do you feel the kingdom of God is benefitting from your gifts? How do you feel society is benefitting from your gifts?

   Corinthians 12:4-6 *There are different kinds of gifts, but the same Spirit distributes them. There are different kinds of service, but the same Lord. There are different kinds of working, but in all of them and in everyone it is the same God at work.*

   Romans 12:6-8 *We have different gifts, according to the grace given to each of us. If your gift is prophesying, then prophesy in accordance with your faith; if it is serving, then serve; if it is teaching, then teach; if it is to encourage, then give encouragement; if it is giving, then give generously; if it is to lead, do it diligently; if it is to show mercy, do it cheerfully.*

   Corinthians 7:7 *I wish that all of you were as I am. But each of you has your own gift from God; one has this gift, another has that.*

# LESSON 9 NOTES

POEM 10

# We Should Leave a Lasting Impact

Amplify my works
to create a seismic shift
felt long after me.

# LESSON 10
# WE SHOULD LEAVE A LASTING IMPACT

*All people are like grass, and all their glory is like the flowers of the field; the grass withers and the flowers fall, but the word of the Lord endures forever.*

1 Peter 1:24-25

Sometimes, I sit on the porch and watch the butterflies dance from flower to flower. They demonstrate such beauty and grace in flight. Some are about the size of my hand, and others are about the size of my fingertip. Some move quickly where I can't possibly catch them, while others stand a chance of my catching them on a good day.

They come in a multitude of colors and all different types. As much as I would love to see these regal creatures year round, unfortunately, they will not last forever. The life cycle of a butterfly moves from egg, to caterpillar (larva), to chrysalis (pupa), and to adult. With all this activity going on, you would think butterflies would be around for a long time. Although the truth is, while a few species may last for nine to twelve months, most butterflies have a reduced life cycle of only two to four weeks after reaching adulthood. But their contribution to future generations lives on long after they fly their last flight.

My mom has always been a beautiful woman, inside and out. Now in her seventies, she doesn't move as fast as she used to and has some health challenges. My mom spent fifty years as an educator, from teaching all grades to becoming a counselor where she spent nearly forty years in that role.

During her time as a counselor, she and a dream team of educators were responsible for shaping a school in the middle of

Chicago, which was new at the time she joined the staff. This school would go on to produce some of the best and brightest students in the Chicago area, most of whom were college-bound and would later go on to have successful careers in their chosen paths.

When my mom retired, the number of teachers, students, and parents who came out to celebrate her was overwhelming. The love, support, and appreciation she received was a testament to all she had poured into each student, each family, and the school during her fifty-year tenure as an educator.

She looked forward to retirement, with plans to improve her bridge card game skills, participate on an engineering board she had worked closely with when she started the school's engineering club, and even substitute teaching to stay connected to education. There's no doubt her legacy will live on for years, maybe even a generation or two beyond the students she interacted with originally. But there will come a time, even with her noteworthy legacy, that her impact on the students will come to an end.

When I think about my lasting impact, I don't think in terms of the work I've done as an engineer or teacher for the school district. Instead, I think of it in terms of what I have done to share God's Word with others. I think about all the students who have gotten baptized after going through children's church. I think about the adults I have worked with as a small group leader, and about being part of the invitation care team where we invite people to accept Christ. Also, I think about my coworkers with whom I share God's love. These are the things that will last for eternity.

All too often we get caught up in thinking our jobs are our reason for being ... we falsely believe our impact will carry on in the company where we so tenaciously dedicated our entire existence. We feel that our title of director, vice president, manager, or lead will somehow keep our legacy alive and well. We think the processes and policies we've put in place will continue to exist after we depart. It may offer that success we crave, but, we must understand that success and impact are two different things.

Success is transactional—how much money did you make, how many deals did you close, and how did you affect the bottom line as a result of your efforts? Then there is impact, which is relational. How many people did you positively influence, how many lives did you change, who were you able to inspire, and did your inspiration cause them to take action to improve the quality of their lives?

To me, the greatest lasting impact we can offer is sharing about God's Word. It is inviting others who may not know who God is, to first see him through us, and then to encourage them to see him for themselves. It is then, eventually, having them accept Jesus' sacrifice for us in their hearts. This is what lasting impact looks like, and we can all have it. Making a difference in others' lives starts with relationship building and sharing God's love, that he sacrificed his son for us.

Who is that person God is calling you to be ... how are you willing to have a lasting impact on humanity and God's kingdom?

1. What do you want your legacy to be?

2. If an account were to be given for the impact you made within your community, what would the account read? Would the community notice if you were gone?

3. What do these scriptures tell you about impact and legacy?

Matthew 9:37-38 *Then he said to his disciples, "The harvest is plentiful but the workers are few. Ask to Lord of the harvest, therefore, to send out workers into his harvest field.*

Acts 20:35 *In everything I did, I showed you that by this kind of hard work we must help the weak, remembering the words the Lord Jesus himself said: 'It is more blessed to give than to receive.'*

John 15:8 *This is to my Father's glory, that you bear much fruit, showing yourselves to be my disciples.*

# LESSON 10 NOTES

## POEM 11

## God Sustains Us When We Are Weary

I've discovered that weary days
come after weary nights.
Nights filled with lingering thoughts
anxiously bleeding into the dawn's first light,
I've known all too well these days and nights.
But blessed are the days where occasionally
a night's respite seems to allow shoulders to drop,
at least for a moment.
A slow, thankful sigh envelopes the air
like when a newborn finally sleeps,
and all is as should be.
Like freshly fallen snow
that sparkles in the moonlight.

# LESSON 11

# GOD SUSTAINS US WHEN WE ARE WEARY

*... but those who hope in the LORD will renew their strength. They will soar on wings like eagles; they will run and not grow weary, they will walk and not be faint.*
Isaiah 40:31

Each year around October, I see the evidence of a long journey nearing its final resting stop as monarchs descend upon Texas cities. Our city is one of many stops along the migration path, where some monarchs travel from as far as southern Canada to reach their destination in Mexico.

For some of these butterflies, this trip is about 3,000 miles. Now I don't know about you, but I don't even want to be in a car for 3,000 miles, let alone flap wings for that long! How do they do it?

By the time they make it to my garden, some of them look, for lack of a better word, dusty ... like they've been through a LOT. Some even come looking like they've been in the ring with a prized fighter, with wings all tattered and, in some cases, torn off in spots. I often wonder what it must be like to be these butterflies ... to just keep going even when it gets rough.

And then I remember **exactly** what it feels like to just keep going, even when it gets rough. That wonderful retirement I spoke of for my mom? Well, it hasn't been as wonderful as planned.

I started to notice memory challenges with my mom. Later, others had started to notice. Shortly after that, the bottom fell out. Not feeling she was in a state where she could maintain her independence, I flew home to check on her. I was met with the toughest time I had ever experienced.

She was not in a good mental or physical state. I also had to take keys from her, which was not easy because she was lucid enough to do everything she wanted, but not fully cognizant to make rational decisions. She even went so far as to have her car towed to the dealership to get extra key fobs synched since she thought she had lost her keys. These were tough times. I was always tiptoeing around to not set her off. At times she felt very low and vulnerable. Through tears and an anguished voice, I would hear her ask, "Why does God hate me?" What she couldn't see was how beautifully God was covering her, all of us, even in these times of immensely painful chaos. My sister and I tried many times to relocate her.

The big break came when my sister flew in, for the third time, determined to get her on the road to where she lived. My sister's neighbor was moving out and allowed her to rent his home. We were also blessed enough to have our aunt say she would come and take care of our mom. Now all we needed to do was, for the third time, try to get her out of the house.

My sister and I planned, packed, and prayed. We gave it ALL to God that evening. We prayed that in the morning, we would be able to get our mom in the car my sister had rented and pull out on the way to my sister's home, several states away. After we prayed, we went to bed.

The next morning, I awoke early and again started praying. God whispered to speak her love language—food! I immediately got up and started to cook breakfast. While I cooked, she came to the top of the stairs. The day before she was forceful and determined she would go NOWHERE. However, this morning, she was different. I told her good morning and asked if she wanted some breakfast. She said happily that she did, but she also said something that rocked me to my core. I told her that today was the day we would leave. She nodded and said, "Please don't leave me." I assured her she would be right with us.

Just wow. The grace and mercy of God shone throughout the house that morning. We nervously awaited the time to pick up our aunt, bring her to the house, get our mom in the car we had packed, and have my mom, sister, and aunt roll out. Even though our mom tried to change her mind at the last minute, we were able to persuade her to leave. Eventually, my sister pulled off and I stayed behind to tend to other matters. I sent a message to my mom's siblings, and we all praised God.

There have been many, many moments past that day where it has been clear that God has been covering and ordering our steps even when we are tired. We later moved my mom fifteen minutes from where I live. I go check on her almost every night to make sure she is loved and cared for. God gives me the strength to show up daily and gives my sister the strength to provide the additional help and support needed. God has been so faithful and has sustained us through so much. It has been a long and tiring road, but we are blessed, still standing, and filled with gratitude.

1. What do you do to keep moving forward when you are weary?

2. How can your faith in God help with a weary mind? What about a weary body?

3. How can you apply these scriptures when your mind, body, or spirit are weary?

   2 Corinthians 12:9 *But he said to me, "My grace is sufficient for you, for my power is made perfect in weakness." Therefore I will boast all the more gladly about my weaknesses, so that Christ's power may rest on me.*

   Psalm 73:26 *My flesh and my heart may fail, but God is the strength of my heart and my portion forever.*

   Galatians 6:9 *Let us not become weary in doing good, for at the proper time we will reap a harvest if we do not give up.*

# LESSON 11 NOTES

# POEM 12

# God Is with Us When We Are Afraid

Come join me my child.
Let me tell you the story of the one who said yes.
Yes to a life more abundant,
Yes to more time with me,
Yes to a deeper understanding,
Yes to taking time to just be.
In my presence she reveled
Of diamonds and glitter.
Her heart said yes, spreading
Sparkles of joy to all who
danced in the rain of thankfulness,
Thankful because she said yes.

# LESSON 12
# GOD IS WITH US WHEN WE ARE AFRAID

*For I am the Lord your God who takes hold of your right hand and says to you, Do not fear; I will help you.*
Isaiah 41:13

I like being close to my butterflies. A little too close for their comfort, honestly. As soon as they sense my presence, they scatter, wildly flying left, right, and up—as if afraid. I'm sure taking flight to avoid potential danger is instinctual, but something interesting happens. They fly over the gate, around the yard, but eventually come back to the flowers they were nectaring on, even with me standing right there.

I think that's how some of us (my hand is raised) handle our encounters with God when we are afraid to do something. We flee, telling ourselves and God that it is too difficult or scary to accomplish. However, if we are wise, even though we are afraid, we recognize that God is present. When we come back to being in his presence, we recognize he is right there, helping us through these moments.

I love public speaking. For me, getting up in front of an audience is exhilarating. It just feels natural ... well, except for the two times when I was terrified to speak. I vividly recall the first time this happened. I write poetry, and up until that point, had never dared to share my poetry with anyone. Any person who is an artist knows what a vulnerable process it is to share your work with the world ... let alone if you are new at your craft, and only your mom has told you how great you are.

I had taken a class at church, which was geared toward empowering us to be the dynamic women we are. At the end of class I decided that to honor my transformation into boldness, I would read some of my poems aloud. I recall looking up the local poetry society, and upon seeing the words "open mic," I was determined to conquer my fear of sharing my poetry out loud.

The day came. I got in my car and set this self-fulfilling prophecy in motion. But there was one huge problem ... I was TERRIFIED. I drove toward the venue, thirty minutes away, crying. Yes, crying. I was so nervous that I was shaking. But I kept driving. I asked God to help me make it through as I drove.

I know I should have prayed and left it at the altar, but I sure enough picked fear back up and carried it all the way into the venue. At the front door, I was welcomed by a person from the poetry society and asked if I wanted to sign up for the open mic. Heart still beating, I said, "Yes."

There I wrote my name as the fourth person on the list to speak and took my seat. There was a main poet who spoke, and a few announcements were made. Then it was time for the open mic portion. The first person went forward and read his poem. Then the next, then the next. Finally, it was my time to get up. I breathed slowly in and out, asked God to help me make it through this moment, and stood up. I walked up, opened my poetry journal to the earmarked page, smiled, and started to read. I had done it!

But I wasn't prepared for what I saw next. I looked into the crowd and saw people wiping tears away. Wait, what? I had spoken about my dad and some challenges he had, but the fact that he was still my dad.

What I learned that day was bigger than saying the poem. I learned that my poetry is a way to connect, inspire, and invite people to be a part of something bigger than myself. I learned that my poetry evokes feelings that allow people to better express their emotions. Since that day, I get up to read my poems every time I can. My most recent poem is one of my favorites. It talks about the essence of our connectedness. I did not hesitate at all to read it. As I hoped, it was well-received.

I have learned something important along this journey of sharing my poetry. My words need to be shared with the world.

Also, I have learned if God's hand is in whatever you do, including reading poetry and writing a book, the words from your mouth to other people's ears will be wrapped in divine language.

I now use my voice wherever I go and share whenever I can. I love when people come up to me afterwards and share how my words moved them, especially when my words move them to act. When I communicate, even afraid ... no, especially afraid, I am glorifying God with my obedience. By leaning on him, the message of his voice flows through me. It is such an exhilarating feeling to use your gifts and walk obediently in the presence of God, even if you do it afraid.

1. Think of a time when you were afraid. How did you make it through that moment?

2. How can times of fear be used to improve your walk with God?

3. How can these scriptures help the next time you experience fear or anxiety?

Isaiah 41:10 *So do not fear, for I am with you; do not be dismayed, for I am your God. I will strengthen you and help you; I will uphold you with my righteous hand.*

Psalm 23:4 *Even though I walk through the darkest valley, I will fear no evil, for you are with me; your rod and your staff, they comfort me.*

Philippians 4:6-7 *Do not be anxious about anything, but in every situation, by prayer and petition, with thanksgiving, present your requests to God. And the peace of God, which transcends all understanding, will guard your hearts and your minds in Christ Jesus.*

# LESSON 12 NOTES

# FROM THE AUTHOR

Thank you for allowing me to share the lessons I have learned from the butterflies in my garden. I hope these experiences have left your heart and spirit feeling the awesome love and power of God as he speaks through nature.

   If there are any thoughts, ideas, or lessons that have helped to enlighten, guide, move, or convict you, please feel free to let me know. I'm on Instagram @krayne95, or I can be reached via email at karmon@dashofcolorvo.com. I'd love to connect. As my last desire for this book, I leave you with a bonus page on how to start your own garden, and some photos I have taken since I began writing. Thank you again for joining me on this journey.

# BONUS PAGE

I have had so many people say to me, "I want to start a butterfly garden, but I don't know what to do/plant." Well fear not! Let's get you started! Google "host plants for butterflies in [city near you]." Host plants are what the caterpillars eat when they hatch from their eggs.

If you are not ready to commit to an actual garden space, you can easily plant a few host plants from your list in some big pots or a raised rectangular wooden planter, as shown in one of the photos that will follow. It really is that easy. That is how I started the first year! In my garden this year, I have the following host plants: milkweed (for monarch caterpillars), red acanthus (for crimson patch caterpillars—new for me!), and fennel (for black swallowtail caterpillars). The year before last I planted a passionflower vine for gulf fritillary caterpillars. They were both beautiful, but be warned, the vine takes over the garden quite rapidly, and gulf fritillary butterflies produce a LOT of caterpillars. There were chrysalises hanging in almost any spot you can think of. It was both amazing and overwhelming for me!

Also get a few flowering plants listed as nectar plants in your area so the butterflies that land in your garden have something to drink. Gregg's mistflower, zinnias, Texas violet salvia (sage), and lantanas are great options where I live. If in-ground, all of these except for zinnias are usually perennials (in Central Texas).

It may seem discouraging at first if you don't see any butterflies, let alone caterpillars, for weeks. But over time, you will be amazed when you start seeing those first little eggs, and shortly after, caterpillars. By the second or third year, your garden will be home to many beautiful butterflies and their babies!

Caution: if you plant fennel for black swallowtail caterpillars, bunnies love that (unfortunately ours in the area love everything). You will have to find a way to put a little fence around that or do like we did this year and put it up off the ground in a planter if you see evidence of sabotage.

Bonus: in addition to butterflies, the following nectaring plants will give you plenty of hummingbirds and all types of bees (bumble, honey, etc.). This is the row order I have in my second garden based on the height they will grow: first row—purple salvia/sage (mentioned earlier), second row —canna lilies (mine have purplish leaves and red flowers), and third row— Esperanza (caution, ours are about 8-10 feet tall, so plant at back of garden by a wall and not blocking windows,).

Also great for bees/butterflies but need space: I planted a lilac vitex. Don't ask me why I thought it would be a shrub. It most certainly is not. It is a tree. But the bees and butterflies love it, even if it does take up a third of my butterfly garden and is seven feet tall.

I hope you have enjoyed these butterfly garden tips! I also hope you will delight in the photos that follow. I love beautifying my little piece of the world while helping butterflies and other pollinators thrive.

# GARDEN AND BUTTERFLY PHOTOS

The images that follow are photographs taken in or near my garden. I hope you enjoy them!

Black swallowtail caterpillar hungrily devouring a fennel shoot

Queen caterpillar feasting on milkweed

Queen chrysalis attached to black fence

Female black swallowtail butterfly

Monarch nearing time to emerge from chrysalis

Common Buckeye butterfly on lilac vitex flower

Bordered patch butterfly perched on Gregg's mistflower

Long-tailed skipper

Butterfly garden made with 2 planters after moving homes

Installation of butterfly garden

Butterfly garden

Installation of second garden

Second garden, preferred by hummingbirds, bees, and many other pollinators

Gulf fritillary in various stages of pupating and forming a chrysalis

Gulf fritillary butterflies mating

Pipevine swallowtail nectaring on Gregg's mistflower

Variegated fritillary nectaring on flowering lilac vitex

Salt Marsh Caterpillar

Salt Marsh Moth resting on a glove

Front view of Salt Marsh Moth

Question mark butterfly

Black swallowtail ready to take its maiden voyage

# ABOUT THE AUTHOR

Karmon Hill is a techie by day and a creative by night. She is a trained voiceover artist, has written and recorded songs, and loves public speaking. Most notable is her participation in Toastmasters where she has held offices and competed in speech competitions. Her dream is to continue competing and eventually win on the world stage of public speaking.

Karmon is a dementia advocate for her mom and is working on an upcoming book that highlights the journey of dementia through the eyes of a caregiver. She has shared her words and wisdom on the subject, having most recently participated as a guest on the *Bereaved But Still Me* podcast. This podcast amplifies the shared experiences of those going through various forms and stages of grieving.

Karmon is also active in her church. She has been an active member in the children's ministry for over fifteen years and serves as a group leader for the church's congregation-wide discipleship initiative.

Karmon currently lives in Texas where she cherishes spending quiet time with her husband and watching the butterflies that frequent their backyard. She is also the proud mom of two college-aged sons.

Relational, intentional, and purpose-filled is how she describes this season of her life.